TOOLS OF THE TRADE

SandCastle
Tools of the Trade

SAWS

ANDERS HANSON

Consulting Editor, Diane Craig, M.A./Reading Specialist

ABDO
Publishing Company

Published by ABDO Publishing Company, 8000 West 78th Street, Edina, Minnesota 55439.

Copyright © 2010 by Abdo Consulting Group, Inc. International copyrights reserved in all countries.

No part of this book may be reproduced in any form without written permission from the publisher. SandCastle™ is a trademark and logo of ABDO Publishing Company.

Printed in the United States.

Editor: Pam Price
Content Developer: Nancy Tuminelly
Cover and Interior Design and Production: Mighty Media
Photo Credits: Shutterstock, iStockphoto (Joseph Abbott, Rob Belknap), JupiterImages Corporation

Library of Congress Cataloging-in-Publication Data
Hanson, Anders, 1980-
  Saws / Anders Hanson.
    p. cm. -- (Tools of the trade)
  ISBN 978-1-60453-584-6
  1. Saws--Juvenile literature. I. Title.

TJ1233.H38 2009
621.9'34--dc22

                            2008055053

SandCastle™ Level: Fluent

SandCastle™ books are created by a team of professional educators, reading specialists, and content developers around five essential components—phonemic awareness, phonics, vocabulary, text comprehension, and fluency—to assist young readers as they develop reading skills and strategies and increase their general knowledge. All books are written, reviewed, and leveled for guided reading, early reading intervention, and Accelerated Reader® programs for use in shared, guided, and independent reading and writing activities to support a balanced approach to literacy instruction. The SandCastle™ series has four levels that correspond to early literacy development. The levels are provided to help teachers and parents select appropriate books for young readers.

Emerging Readers
(no flags)

Beginning Readers
(1 flag)

Transitional Readers
(2 flags)

Fluent Readers
(3 flags)

SandCastle™ would like to hear from you. Please send us your comments and suggestions.
sandcastle@abdopublishing.com

CONTENTS

chain saw

WHAT IS A SAW?

A saw is a cutting tool. Saws have lots of sharp points called teeth. To make a cut, move the saw back and forth across the **material** that needs cutting. Saws should be harder than the material they cut into. Otherwise, the sharp teeth will quickly dull.

HISTORY

Metal saws have been around for about 4,500 years. Before that, people made simple sawlike tools out of stone.

The ancient Egyptians used metal handsaws to cut wood.

The first circular saw was invented about 200 years ago.

circular
saw blade

ancient
stone saw

HANDSAW

There are different kinds of teeth for cutting different **materials.**

Sawing by hand is hard work. Some saws can be used by two people.

There are many types of handsaws.

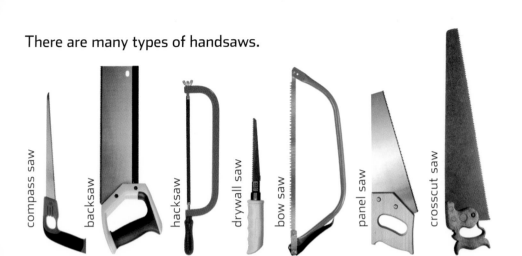

compass saw

backsaw

hacksaw

drywall saw

bow saw

panel saw

crosscut saw

Handsaws are operated by hand.

Jim cuts through wood with a handsaw.
He is building a swing set for his niece.

Dave uses a handsaw to cut a wooden **plank**.
He is building a large office.

CIRCULAR SAW

Some circular saws can be *mounted* on tables.

circular saw blades

Each blade is **designed** to cut a different kind of **material**.

A circular saw cuts by spinning a round saw blade very fast.

Circular saws are excellent tools for making straight cuts. They are powered by electricity.

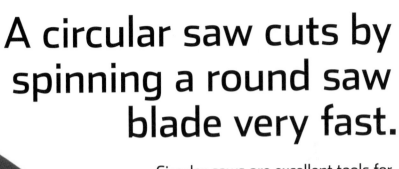

18.0v

18.0v

battery

power cord

Ted uses a circular saw to cut through metal. He is making a shelf for his friend.

Damon saws wood with a circular saw.
He **adjusted** his saw to cut at an angle.

CHAIN SAW

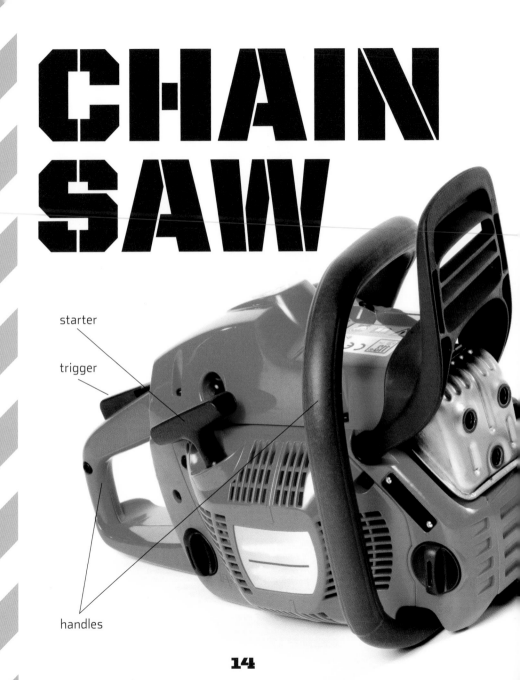

starter

trigger

handles

A chain saw has a chain with many small blades.

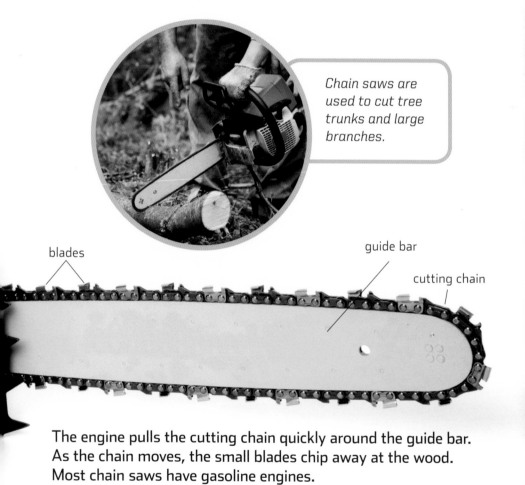

Chain saws are used to cut tree trunks and large branches.

blades

guide bar

cutting chain

The engine pulls the cutting chain quickly around the guide bar. As the chain moves, the small blades chip away at the wood. Most chain saws have gasoline engines.

James saws through wood with a chain saw.
He is cutting through a tree stump.

Chain saws can be used to make art too.
This artist is working on a bear **sculpture**.

JIGSAW

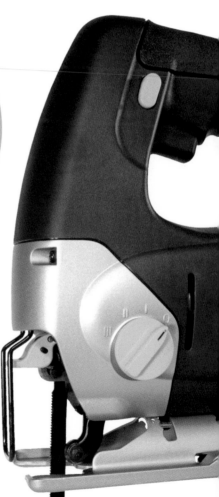

Sawdust goes flying as a jigsaw cuts through wood.

Jigsaws can use different types of blades.

18

Jigsaws are used to make curved cuts.

A jigsaw has a small, thin blade that moves up and down. The blade bends to make smooth, curved cuts.

The curved body of an electric guitar could be cut with a jigsaw.

The teeth face outward.

Albert is cutting a **plank** of wood.
He makes a curved cut with a jigsaw.

A jigsaw has a metal plate on its bottom. The plate rests on the **material** being cut.

MATCH GAME

Match the words to the pictures! The answers are on the bottom of the page.

1. chain saw   A.

2. jigsaw   B.

3. handsaw   C.

4. circular saw   D.

TOOL QUIZ

Test your tool knowledge with this quiz!
The answers are on the bottom of the page.

1. Handsaws use electricity.
   True or false?

2. Circular saws have round
   blades. True or false?

3. Chain saws are not used to
   cut through tree trunks.
   True or false?

4. Jigsaws have small, thin
   blades. True or false?

GLOSSARY

adjust – to change something slightly to produce a desired result.

design – to plan how something will appear or work.

material – the substance something is made of, such as metal, fabric, or plastic.

mount – to set in a raised position.

plank – a thick, heavy board, usually at least two inches thick and eight inches wide.

sculpture – a three-dimensional work of art.